MW01038994

Carol Wingert

Eagle Vision Media

920 Franklin Ave

Connellsville, PA 15425

Printed in the United States of America

WARNING!

Use this book at your own risk. Take your time, be absolutely positive about anything that goes into your mouth. The world of edible plants is wonderful, if you take the time to positively identify the plants you are studying, learn how to avoid poisonous plants, and get in touch with your body so that you notice how each plant effects you.

Enjoy,

Carol Wingert

http://www.carolwingert.com

http://www.iphotographgod.com

Table of Contents

ASIATIC DAYFLOWER (commelina communis)

Young leaves and stems

Use – Salad & Cooked Greens

Young leaves and stems can be added fresh to salads, or boiled for 10 minutes and served

Bull Thistle (cirsium vulgare)

Young leaves, young stems and roots

Uses – Salad, cooked greens, cooked vegetables

With spines removed, young leaves can be added to salads, or cooked as greens.

Pithy young stems are excellent peeled and eaten raw or cooked.

Raw or cooked roots of first year plants (without stems) are great survival food.

Burdock (arctium minus)

Young leaves, roots

Uses – cooked greens, cooked vegetables, salad, candy

Tender young leaves – added to salads or boiled in several changes of water.

Roots – once the thick inedible rind is removed, the roots of the first year plants can be boiled for 30 minutes (in two changes of water) and served with butter.

Cattails (typda latifolia)

Young shoots & stalks, immature flower spikes, pollen, sprouts, rootstock

Uses – Salad, asparagus, cooked vegetables, flour, pickle, potato.

Young shoots, young spring stalks – peeled to the white core & eaten raw or cooked.

Immature flower spikes - gather before they erupt and boiled for a few minutes. Serve with butter and eat like corn on the cob.

Pollen can be gathered to make an excellent protein-rich flour (mix half and half with wheat flour.)

Late summer, the horn-shape sprout can be added to salads or boined for 10 minutes and served with butter.

One of the best and most versatile of our native edible plants!

Common Chickweed (stellaria media)

Tender leaves and stems

Uses – Salads, cooked greens

Tender leaves and stems can be added to salads, but bet if boiled for 5 minutes and served as a green.

Chicory (cichorium intybus)

Young leaves and roots

Uses – Coffee, salad, cooked greens

Roots – roast in oven till dark brown & brittle, grind and prepare like coffee.

Above ground part, boiled 5-10 minutes

White underground parts of young leaves are great in salads.

Dandelion (taraxacum officinale)

Young leaves, flower-buds, flowers, roots

Use – Salad, cooked greens, cooked vegetable, fritters, coffee

Young leaves before flowers appear, added to salads, or boiled for 10-15 minutes.

Flower-buds can be boiled and served with butter, or pickled.

Flowers are excellent dipped in batter and fried.

Coffee like beverage – bake the roots in a slow oven until brown and brittle, grind and perk like regular coffee.

Day-Lily (hemerocallis fulva)

Young shoots, flower-buds, flowers, tubers

Uses – Salad, asparagus, cooked vegetable, fritters, seasoning

Early shoots – add to salads or prepare like asparagus.

Young flower buds, prepare like green beans or when older, fritters.

Fresh flowers – Fritters, or used fresh, withered or dried to season stews.

Tubers (early) add to salads, or prepare like corn. Older tubers can be prepared like corn.

Garlic Mustard (alliaria petiolate)

Leaves, flowers

Uses – Salads and Pestos

Young leaves – great in salad with other wild greens, or cooked greens. (I put the leaves in the rice cooker with a few cups of rice, and wild onions – great meal!)

Flowers – put in salads, or cooked with leaves and other greens.

Ground Ivy aka Gill-over-the-ground (glechoma hederacea)

Leaves

Uses – Tea

Leaves – dried leaves make a fine herbal tea, steep for 5-10 minutes in hot water.

Jewel Weed aka Pale Touch-me-not (impatiens pallida)

Young stems, shoots and leaves

Uses – cooked greens, remedy fro Poison Ivy & Nettles

Young shoots (up to 6 inches) – boil in 2 changes of water for 10-15 minutes. Serve as a cooked green. (DO NOT drink the cooking water)

Stems and leaves – crush to get the juice. It sooths the sting of nettles, and has been know to prevent poison ivy.

May Apple aka Mandrake (podophyllum peltatum)

Mature fruit ONLY

Uses- fresh fruit, jelly, cold drink.

e large pale yellow berries ripen as the plants begin to wither & die.

The pulp surrounding the seeds can be eaten raw, or cooked and made into jelly. The juice can be added lemonade

WARNING: THE ROOTS, LEAVES, FLOWERS, SEEDS AND GREEN FRUIT ARE STRONGLY CATHARTIC AND **SHOULD NOT BE EATEN.**

Milkweed (asclepias syriaca)

Young shoots, leaves, unopened flower buds, flowers, young pods

Uses – Asparagus, cooked greens, cooked vegetable, fritters

Cover the young shoots (up to 6 inches) with boiling water, cook for 15 minutes, using several changes of water. First few changes should be fairly rapid with just over a minute between changes. **Be sure to use boiling water when making each change.** The young top leaves, flowerbuds, and small young pods are prepared the same way.

Flowers – can be dipped into boiling water for 1 minute, covered with batter and fried to make fritters

Warning:

Do not confuse young shoots with those of Dogbane or Butterfly weed. Milkweed shoots – downy-hairy with milky sap. Dogbane – hairless. Butterfly weed lacks milky sap

Wood Nettle (laportea canadensis)

Young shoots and leaves

Uses – cooked greens, soup, tea

Young shoots and tender pale green top leaves – simmer 10-15 minutes in just enough water to cover. Serve with butter. Add to soups and stews. For tea, boil shoots or leaves for several minutes, strain, and add sugar/lemon to taste.

Warning – Do NOT handle with bear hands, but if you do come in contact with the stinging hairs, rub the area with crushed stems from the jewelweed.

Nodding Wild Onion (allium cernuum)

Leaves, underground bulb

Use – cooked vegetables, pickle, salad, seasoning, cooked greens.

Underground bulbs – boiled, pickled, added to salads or used as a seasoning.

Tender leaves (before stocks appear) – cook as greens along with the bulbs, or add raw to salads.

Ox-eye Daisy (chrysanthemum leucanthemum)

Young leaves

Uses – Salad

Tender young leaves (lighter green) make an interesting addition to a salad.

Common Plantain (plantago major)

Young leaves

Uses – Salad, cooked greens

Chop and add to salads. Boil for 10-15 minutes and add butter.

Gather while very young as the older leaves will be to stringy for use.

Common Evening Primrose (oenothera biennis)

Young leaves and roots

Uses – Cooked vegetables, salad, cooked greens

First year taproots – peel and boil 20-30 minutes in 2 or 3 changes of water and serve with butter.

Fresh roots are peppery, but become milder during certain times of the year, usually late fall or early spring.

Tender new leaves – peel and serve as a peppery addition to salads or boil for 20 minutes in 2 or 3 changes of water and serve with butter. Slightly bitter but palatable.

Purple Dead Nettle (lamium purpureum)

Young plant tops and leaves

Uses – Salads and in a stirfry as a spring vegetable.

Flowers and leaves can be boiled for 20-30 minute, drain, then season to taste.

(I've mixed these with other greens in my rice dishes)

Queen Anne's Lace aka Wild Carrot (daucus carota)

Roots

Uses – Cooked vegetables

Roots, white and smell like carrots – Prepare the first year roots like garden carrots.

Warning: Early leaves resemble Poison Hemlock, only stems are hairy.

Red Clover (trifolium pratense)

Young leaves and flower heads

Uses – Salad, cooked greens, flour and tea

Flowerheads and young leaves are difficult to digest raw, but can be eaten in quantity if soaked fro several hours in salty water or boiled for 5-10 minutes.

Dried flowerheads make a great healthy tea.

Dried flowerheads and seeds can be ground into a nutritious flour.

Clover is very abundant and rich in protein.

Spring Beauties (claytonia virginica)

Corms

Use – potato

Corms– excellent, but very tedious to gather in larger quantities. Boil for 10-15 minutes, strip off the tough outer jackets and serve with butter.

Staghorn Sumac (rhus typhina)

Fruit

Use – Cold Drink

Fruit – when ripe the berries are covered with acidic red hairs. Collect the entire cluster, rub gently to bruise the berries, and soak for 10-15 minutes in COLD water. Remove the cluster, pour the pink juice through cheesecloth to strain the hairs and any loose berries. Sweeten to taste and chill.

White Trillium (trillium grandiflorum)
Very young leaves

Use – Salad, cooked greens

Young unfolding leaves are great in salads tasting like raw sunflower seeds.

Boil leaves for 10 minutes and serve with vinegar.

*leaves become bitter once the buds and flowers appear.

** most trilliums should not be picked but are occasionally found in sufficient quantity to warrant collection.

Violet (viola papilionacea)

Young leaves and Flowers

Use – salads, cooked greens, soup thickener, tea and candy

Greens can be cooked for 10-15 minutes or added to soup. Dried leaves can be made into tea.

Flowers can be candied.

Yarrow (achillea millefolium)

Leaves

Uses – Tea

Steep the dried leaves 10-15 minutes.

Wild Bergamot (monarda fistulosa)

Leaves and flowerheads

Use – Tea

Steep fresh or dried leaves and flowerheads for 10 minutes, and sweeten to taste.   Excellent mixed with other teas.